March Journal Jumpstarts

A Month of Creative Writing Prompts

Written by
Cindy Barden

Editors: Barbara G. Hoffman and Michael Batty

Cover and Interior Design: Good Neighbor Press, Inc.

Illustrator: Chris Nye

FS112136 March Journal Jumpstarts

All rights reserved—Printed in the U.S.A.
23740 Hawthorne Boulevard
Torrance, CA 90505-5927

Notice! Pages may be reproduced for classroom or home use only, not for commercial resale. No part of this publication may be reproduced for storage in a retrieval system or transmitted in any form or by any means—electronic, mechanical, recording, etc.—without the prior permission of the publisher. Reproduction of these materials for an entire school or school system is strictly prohibited.

Copyright © 2000 Frank Schaffer Publications, Inc.

Table of Contents
March

Introduction 1
March on Mars 2
Picture, Picture 3
Borrowing 4
Favorite Flower 5
Nifty Inventions 6
Animal Races 7
Long Lines 8
Anything Else 9
Yes! 10
Hello, Mr. President 11
Name Change 12
Think Drink 13
Shop Talk 14
Finders Keepers? 15
Flutter By, Butterfly 16
Night Sight 17
Happy St. Patrick's Day 18
Marvelous Mondays 19
Fly like a Bird 20
Spring is Near 21
Let's Celebrate! 22
Magic Show 23
Seeing Red 24
Captain Kid 25
Hickory, Dickory, Dock 26
Changes 27
Stuffed Animals 28
I Am Proud of Myself 29
Letters Tell All 30

© Frank Schaffer Publications, Inc.   FS112136 March Journal Jumpstarts

Introduction

An empty journal is filled with infinite possibilities.

Writing regularly in a journal helps us to develop our imaginations, encourages us to express our thoughts, feelings, and dreams, and provides a way to communicate experiences in words and pictures. Many students feel frustrated when asked to keep a journal. They may not be sure of what to write, or they may be intimidated by a blank sheet of paper. Even professional writers occasionally face "writer's block." The Journal Jumpstarts series provides ideas and suggestions for daily journal entries. Each book contains 29 jumpstarts. You could give each student a photocopy of the same page or provide a variety of pages and allow students to choose their own topics. You may have students who will be able to sit and write without jumpstarts. At times students may prefer to express their thoughts through drawings or with a combination of drawings and writing. Be encouraging!

Through making regular entries in journals, students become more observant of themselves and the world around them. Journal writing on a regular basis strengthens students' attention spans and abilities to focus. Keeping journals promotes self-esteem because students are doing something for themselves—not for grades or in competition with others. A journal can become an essential friend, a confidante in times of personal crisis.

Encourage students to get into the journal habit by setting aside writing time every day at about the same time, such as first thing in the morning or shortly before lunch. Share their journal time by writing in your own journal. What better way to encourage a good habit than by example!

Note: Assure students that what they write is confidential. Provide a safe, secure place for students to store their journals. Respect their privacy, as you would expect your privacy to be respected—read their journals by invitation only.

Name _____   Date _____

March on Mars

The month of March and the planet Mars both get their names from Mars, the Roman god of war and farming. Write about what it would be like to spend this March on the planet Mars. Make up any story that you like.

Name _____ Date _____

Picture, Picture

Think about one of your favorite picture books. Describe three pictures in the book.

FS112136 March Journal Jumpstarts © Frank Schaffer Publications, Inc.

Name _____ Date _____

Borrowing

Has anyone ever borrowed something from you without asking, or borrowed something and forgotten to return it to you? Tell how it made you feel.

Name _____ Date _____

Favorite Flower

What is your favorite kind of flower? Write about why you like that kind best.

_____
_____
_____
_____
_____
_____
_____
_____
_____
_____
_____
_____
_____
_____
_____
_____
_____
_____

Name _____ Date _____

Nifty Inventions

All of the things that we use every day were invented by someone, including pens, pencils, zippers, paper clips, rulers, buttons, tape, scissors, and silverware. Write about one small item that you use almost every day and describe how it's useful to you. How would your life be different without it?

Name _____   Date _____

Animal Races

People race all kinds of animals—horses, dogs, pigs, and even frogs. What would be the strangest kind of animal to race? Write a story describing the kind of race that you come up with. You can even name and enter your own contestant!

_____
_____
_____
_____
_____
_____
_____
_____
_____
_____
_____
_____
_____
_____
_____
_____
_____
_____
_____

Name _____ Date _____

Long Lines

The telephone is a marvelous invention. It allows us to talk directly to people all over the world. If you could call a person living in a faraway place, who would it be? Where would he or she live?

Name _____ Date _____

Anything Else

Write about something that you would rather be doing than writing in this journal. Describe where you are, who is with you, and anything else that comes to mind.

_____
_____
_____
_____
_____
_____
_____
_____
_____
_____
_____
_____
_____
_____
_____

Name _____ Date _____

Yes!

Describe what you like most about yourself and tell why.

_____
_____
_____
_____
_____
_____
_____
_____
_____
_____
_____
_____
_____
_____
_____
_____
_____
_____
_____
_____

© Frank Schaffer Publications, Inc.	**10**	FS112136 March Journal Jumpstarts
reproducible

Name _____   Date _____

Hello, Mr. President

If you could talk to George Washington, the first President of the United States, what would you say?

Name _____   Date _____

Name Change

If you could change your name, what would you call yourself? Explain why you would choose that name.

_____
_____
_____
_____
_____
_____
_____
_____
_____
_____
_____
_____
_____
_____
_____
_____

© Frank Schaffer Publications, Inc.   FS112136 March Journal Jumpstarts

Name _____ Date _____

Think Drink

What's your favorite drink? Write about the drink that you enjoy most. Try to describe what you like about it.

_____
_____
_____
_____
_____
_____
_____
_____
_____
_____
_____
_____
_____
_____
_____
_____
_____

Name _____ Date _____

Shop Talk

Describe what you like most and least about shopping with your parents.

Name _____ Date _____

Finders Keepers?

You find a $20 bill on the floor at the mall. What will you do with it?

Name _____ Date _____

Flutter By, Butterfly

Monarch butterflies migrate every year. They winter in Mexico and fly north in the spring. Imagine that you are a Monarch butterfly flying north. Describe what you see and think as you head toward your summer home.

_____
_____
_____
_____
_____
_____
_____
_____
_____
_____
_____
_____
_____
_____

Name _____ Date _____

Night Sight

Pretend that you are looking at the night sky and see something strange or unexpected. What do you see? Describe it and tell how you feel.

Name _____   Date _____

Happy St. Patrick's Day

Green is the color of St. Patrick's Day. Think about things of yours that are green. Write about your favorite green item and explain why you like it.

_____
_____
_____
_____
_____
_____
_____
_____
_____
_____
_____
_____
_____
_____
_____
_____
_____
_____

Name _____ Date _____

Marvelous Mondays

Write about Mondays in school or at home.
What do you like most about Mondays?
What do you like least?

_____

_____

_____

_____

_____

_____

_____

_____

_____

_____

_____

_____

_____

_____

_____

_____

_____

_____

Name _____ Date _____

Fly like a Bird

If you could be a kind of bird, which kind would you like to be? Write about what you think it would be like to be that kind of bird.

Name _____ Date _____

Spring Is Near

Spring may be just around the corner. Write about what spring is like where you live. Describe the sights, sounds, smells, tastes, and feel of spring.

Name _____ Date _____

Let's Celebrate!

Pretend that today is a holiday called "National Goof-Off Day!" What might you or other people do to celebrate? Describe your day off.

_____
_____
_____
_____
_____
_____
_____
_____
_____
_____
_____
_____
_____
_____
_____
_____
_____

Name _____ Date _____

Magic Show

You and a friend decide to give a magic show. Describe the magic tricks that you will perform to astound the audience!

Name _____ Date _____

Seeing Red

Sometimes we say that a person is "seeing red" when he or she gets angry. Why do you think those words were chosen to describe anger? What makes you see red?

Name _____   Date _____

Captain Kid

Pretend that you are the captain of a ship. Write the name of your ship and describe where you might go.

Name _____ Date _____

Hickory, Dickory, Dock

Think about the Mother Goose nursery rhymes that you learned when you were younger. Write about the one that you liked best and tell why you liked it.

_____
_____
_____
_____
_____
_____
_____
_____
_____
_____
_____
_____
_____
_____
_____
_____
_____

Name _____ Date _____

Changes

Think of ways that you have changed over the past year or two. Describe how you have changed.

_____
_____
_____
_____
_____
_____
_____
_____
_____
_____
_____
_____
_____
_____
_____
_____

Name _____ Date _____

Stuffed Animals

Stuffed animal toys are shaped like different kinds of real animals: bears, cats, seals, and others. What would be the strangest kind of animal to make into a stuffed toy? Describe the toy and tell whether you'd want one.

_____
_____
_____
_____
_____
_____
_____
_____
_____
_____
_____
_____
_____
_____
_____
_____

© Frank Schaffer Publications, Inc.　　　　　FS112136 March Journal Jumpstarts

Name _____   Date _____

I Am Proud of Myself

Write about the best thing that you have ever done. Explain why it is important to you and why you are proud of having done it.

Name _____   Date _____

Letters Tell All

Write your name down the lines below, with one letter at the beginning of each line. Skip a line or two between each letter. After each letter write words or phrases that begin with that letter and describe you.